Iniquity

Workbook Study Guide

Voice of The Light Ministries

Iniquity

Workbook Study Guide

Dr. Ana Méndez Ferrell

I am greatly weighed down within my soul as I observe thousands and hundreds of thousands of Christians suffering greatly, going through never-ending deserts, bearing sicknesses with no apparent relief and burdened by irrevocable curses. This suffering has caused me to intensely seek God's face in order to find a solution to so many unanswerable questions.

For many years, God has raised me as a pioneer in a number of areas, spiritual warfare being one of them at the personal and territorial deliverance level. As I have invaded these terrains and stood against the powers of darkness, I have realized that I need to comprehend God's righteousness in a deeper way. The only force that destroys the power of the devil is the righteousness manifested on the cross of Calvary, which is much greater than the simple justification by grace preached in most churches. Through this study, God wants us to discover the wonderful treasures hidden in Jesus Christ, so as to enter the fullness of life found in the depths of the mystery of the cross alone. God wants us to understand "iniquity" as the greatest obstacle to possessing the riches of His glory. Our ignorance about iniquity binds us to curses from which we cannot escape.

In His Word, God makes a specific distinction between sin and iniquity. The Church is used to dealing with the topic of sin to some degree, but almost never touches the vast problem of iniquity. Most Christians are unaware of its existence, so they are unable to be freed from it. Nevertheless, iniquity is one of the most significant topics in the Bible. Ignorance and a lack of understanding about iniquity result in the greatest source of failure, oppression, and defeat that God's people face.

Dr. Ana Mendez Ferrell

Author of the book, "Iniquity".

Voice of The Light Ministries

Iniquity Workbook Study Guide.
2nd Edition 2017.

All scripture quotations unless otherwise indicated are taken from The King James Version.

Category: Educational/Deliverance.

Printing: United States of America.

Published by: Voice of The Light Ministries
P. O. Box 3418
Ponte Vedra, Florida, 32004
United States of America

www.VoiceOfTheLight.com

ISBN-13: 978-1-933163-91-8

Content

INTRODUCTION

1) What is the only thing that destroys the power of the Devil?

a) The righteousness manifested on the cross of Calvary
b) Going to church and following their rules

2) One of the greatest obstacles preventing us from possessing the riches of His glory is:

a) Sin
b) Rebellion
c) Iniquity

CHAPTER 1
WHAT IS INIQUITY?

3) What is iniquity? Mark the correct answer(s) with an X.

a) ___ Anything that turns away from God's perfect and straight path
b) ___ Our sins and transgressions
c) ___ The spiritual DNA, inheritance of evil, imprinted and established at birth and passed on to the next generation
d) ___ What the Bible calls "the body of sin"
e) ___ The evil seed that originates all evil, transmitted to humans from birth
f) ___ The sum of all twisted thoughts, total of all that is evil in mankind

4) Evil is the diabolic seed from which all wickedness originates, transmitted to man in birth, impregnating the heart with thoughts and intentions opposed to everything God is.

a) True
b) False

5) What was the origin of iniquity?

a) ___The sin of disobedience committed by Adam and Eve, following the suggestion of Lucifer, to eat from the tree of the knowledge of good and evil.
b) ___The fall of Lucifer, the archangel, in the moment he allowed a thought that was out of line with God, and started to believe in something different and opposite to Divine Justice.
6) ___Iniquity is a "spiritual substance" that produces evil.

a) True
b) False

7) The words evil and iniquity are synonymous.

a) True
b) False

8) Iniquity carries, from the moment of conception, all information or spiritual inheritance of evil.

a) True
b) False

9) The "body of sin" originates in the spirit and invades the body and soul.

a) True
b) False

10) Iniquity is the source of Satan's legal right to rob and oppress us. This is what prevents us from receiving the full blessings of God.

a) True
b) False

11) Concupiscence (lust and greed) are:

a) Inflicted perverse desires that permeate the human heart and corrupt the soul.
b) An evil seed that originates all evil.

12) Iniquity is the main door that Satan uses to affect the life of a human being that is a:

a) Believer
b) Non-believer
c) Both

13) Iniquity becomes an irresistible force compelling good people to commit abominable sins.

a) True
b) False

14) God visits the _______ of the fathers upon the children bringing judgment.

a) Sin
b) Rebellion
c) Iniquity

15) Trials, tribulations and times in the desert are continuous divine actions to pull the person back to the Father's divine order.

a) True
b) False

16) We can be free of iniquity, only through deep repentance of our sins in the name of Jesus.

a) True
b) False

17) Complete the blanks with key words on page 16.

God does not deal with evil in a ______________________________ manner. He is extremely ______________________________________, and so we must respond to the kingdom of darkness.

God wants us to examine our ____________________________, as well as to understand evil and its consequences in the same dimension He does. He does not want the devil to have something to ____.

18) In Isaiah 53:4,5 and 10, 11, we can see how His sacrifice on the cross touches several areas in which we must be released and redeemed, such as illness, pain, rebellion, evil, sin and affliction of spirit.

a) True
b) False

19) In Leviticus 16:21, it shows that only through specific confession of our sins, transgressions and iniquities can we be washed clean by our Lord.

a) True
b) False

20) Draw a line to the correct meaning:

a) Voluntary iniquity	Root of all sins committed that still tempts us.
b) Conscious iniquity	With all knowledge and desire to practice evil.
c) Unconscious iniquity	Difficult to detect. Can come from past gernerations causing disease and other calamity.

21) Man is spirit, soul and body and must be understood as a whole.

a) True
b) False

22) Millions of Christians have failed to experience victory due to their limited knowledge of the two fundamental parts of man; soul and spirit.

a) True
b) False

23) According to these biblical verses, do you believe there is a "spiritual contamination" that must be cleansed and sanctified in all three parts of our being as believers?

Having therefore these promises, dearly beloved, let us cleanse ourselves from all filthiness of the flesh and spirit, perfecting holiness in the fear of God. 2 Corinthians 7:1

And the very God of peace sanctify you wholly; and I pray God your whole spirit and soul and body be preserved blameless unto the coming of our Lord Jesus Christ. 1 Thessalonians 5:23

a) Yes
b) No

24) Which part of the Spirit corresponds to the following definitions: (Mark only one answer.)

A. Receives revelation from God.
Manifests the gifts of healing, prophecy and words of knowledge.
Detects what is happening in the invisible realm.

____Communion ____ Mind of the Spirit _____Intuition

B. There are various parts: understanding, spiritual intelligence and wisdom of God.
This is where the knowledge of God rests, supernaturally receiving from Him.
This is the place where God reveals the great mysteries of science, for the righteous and the unrighteous.

____Senses of the Spirit ____The Seat of Power _____The Mind of the Spirit

C. Our spirit is united with God to hear Him clearly.
The Lordship of Jesus Christ is established, directing and reigning in our lives and is the governing place of our spiritual being.
Intimacy manifests through the Holy Spirit allowing entrance into the spiritual world where hidden treasures of God are revealed.
Cental part of our spiritual body, Holy of Holies of our temple.

____Communion ____Consciousness ____The Mind of the Spirit

D. The power of God resides in this area of our spirit.
Manifestation of the gifts of miracles, healings and wonders of God come from this part of our spirit.
We become the extension of the hand of God with His power.

____The Seat of Power ____The Mind of the Spirit ____Communion

E. This area is intimately linked to the Heart of Man.
This part awoke when man ate from the tree of knowledge of good and evil, knowing right from wrong.
Houses the "fear of God" and the wisdom of God.

____Spiritual Inheritance ____Communion _____Consciousness

F. Helps us differentiate the origin of things we perceive, being from God or the darkness, spiritual discernment.
These are connected to senses of the soul and compliment one other.
Spiritual hearing, seeing, feeling, smelling, touching help to preceive the invisible world.

____Intuition _____The Seat of Power ____Spiritual Senses

G. Intangible element that records all the spiritual information (DNA)from generation to generation, named iniquity.
God provided us redemption, found in the Spirit of Christ.

____Spiritual Inheritance _____Mind of the Spirit ____Consciousness

Check for all the correct answers in the last section of this workbook. (Page 61)

NOTES

CHAPTER 2
THE CONFLICT BETWEEN THE TWO SEEDS

25) Explain in your own words the meaning of iniquity.

____
____
____

26) List the two seeds which based on Genesis 3:15 are in constant conflict, and describe the nature of each.

____
____
____

27) The divine seed is engendered in us from the moment of our conception.

a) True
b) False

28) When we receive the divine seed in us, an internal conflict begins between the flesh, and the seed of life that has just been spawned upon receiving Christ into our lives.

a) True
b) False

29) Put an X in the correct answer or answers. The flesh is:

a) ____ Where all the spiritual heritage of lawlessness is poured into us.
b) ____ A seed engendered in us that activates sin.
c) ____ The "structure" that leads us away from God's justice.
d) ____ Our "internal" formation as fallen creatures.
e) ____ Evidence of Iniquity manifested.

30) We must purge Iniquity, otherwise it will continuously feed the life of the flesh, making us enemies of God, and invading us with death.

a) True
b) False

31) Iniquity prevents the development of an effective spiritual life.

a) True
b) False

32) Eliminating the sins and desires of the flesh requires much more than a superficial exercise.

a) True
b) False

33) Describe, according to the teachings, the meaning of "walking in the Spirit."

____
____
____
____
____
____

34) Complete the blanks with the keywords on page 40.

It is not man's will which destroys the works of the flesh; but__________________________
It is the seed of God destroying the demonic seed in the flesh. This is only accomplished by the understanding of the ____________________ and spending time in _______________with God.

35) From page 41, explains how religion affects the works of the flesh.

____
____
____
____
____
____

36) From page 41- 42, describe some "bonds of iniquity" which dull effective development of the Spirit.

____
____
____
____
____
____

37) The devil rules in our lives through iniquity, invading our lives with religion, and killing the life of the Spirit.

a) True
b) False

38) In the intangible ways of the Spirit, we can not control what will happen, nor define it in words or rational explanations.

a) True
b) False

39) In Romans 8:1-2 Apostle Paul mentions there are two laws that oppose each other. What are they?

____
____
____
____
____
____

40) When there is iniquity in a believer his growth is slow. He will manifest negativity and his faith will alternate between highs and lows, and even zero. Iniquity always brings feelings of guilt and pressure, filling him with fear and death.

a) True
b) False

41) From page 44, what is the objective of iniquity?

____
____
____
____
____
____

42) A spiritual person is satisfied with giving God a large ministry.

a) True
b) False

43) Complete the blanks, from Romans 8:5-7.

For they that are after the flesh__________________________; but they that are after the Spirit the things of the Spirit. For to be carnally minded is________________________; but to be spiritually minded is __________________ and ________________. Because the carnal mind is________________against God: for it is not subject to the law of God, neither indeed can be.

44) One cannot be of the Spirit and the flesh at the same time. You are one or the other.

a) True
b) False

45) The theory you can live in the flesh and in the spirit at the same time, since God's righteousness justifies us no matter how we live, has infiltrated the church.

a)True
b)False

Check for all the correct answers in the last section of this workbook. (Page 61)

NOTES

CHAPTER 3
THE DWELLINGS OF INIQUITY

46) The soul of Adam was created to dwell in God, in a heavenly abode.

a) True
b) False

47) Define the elements of the spiritual seat of Adam, through which he could rule the earth with the thinking and mind of His Creator.

a) ____________________
b) ____________________
c) ____________________
d) ____________________
e) ____________________
f) ____________________

48) Our Creator left in the hands of Adam a tool to rule, which no one could use, neither God nor the Devil. What is that tool?

____
____
____
____
____
____
____
____

49) The woman lost the right to rule, using her own will to enter the realm "proposed" by the Devil.

a) True
b) False

50) Adam and Eve lost the power to rule, but their spirits did not lose their spiritual dwelling. Their souls continued united with God, but they lost their eternal life.

a) True
b) False

51) Describe the structures of wickedness in which the fallen soul builds his spiritual habitat.

____
____
____
____
____
____
____

52) Which Psalm and verse mentions the existence of these structures of wickedness?

____
____
____

53) The structures of iniquity control, dominate, and fill with woes the societies in which fallen man lives.

a) True
b) False

54) After the fall of man, God stopped reigning over the earth through his children, allowing the devil and death to reign through iniquity.

a) True
b) False

55) The behavior of man is consistent with his spiritual state. For example, in the case of King Nebuchadnezzar, God judged his pride and iniquity and the King adopted an animal mentality in which he became captive.

a) True
b) False

56) Complete the blanks with key words from page 50.

These dwellings of iniquity are ____________________, ____________________ or ____________________ structures from which we operate and from where we make decisions that do not come ____________________.

57) We could say that a structure is an invisible mold around our soul that gives it form, personality and identity.

a) True
b) False

58) Thought structures and emotions have been edified in the mind and heart since childhood and are the result of iniquity.

a) True
b) False

59) We can destroy these structures of iniquity with the phrase: "Lord, Lord, come and live in my heart", thus accepting Christ into our lives and being automatically restored.

a) True
b) False

60) Mark the answer which indicates how we can eliminate the structures of iniquity.

a) ___ By the power of God
b) ___ By our determination and faith to demolish them
c) ___ Changing lies for God's unlimited truth
d) ___ Beginning to think differently about ourselves
e) ___ With a deep and sincere prayer when we receive Christ in our lives
f) ___ Submitting our will to God
g) ___ Seeing ourselves in the grandeur and power with which God sees us, and acting in this way, without doubt
h) ___ Recognizing that these structures of iniquity reside in us, and are controlling our lives
i) ___ Asking a minister on a Sunday in church, to lay hands on us and pray

61) In alphabetical order, write the 15 structures of iniquity listed in the teaching.

62) Explain in your own words what would happen if a man living in poverty and scarcity begins to walk with Christ, receiving deliverance and inner healing but does not break down the structure of poverty and deprivation in his life.

____
____
____
____
____
____

63) In your own words, describe an example of a Christian life living in iniquity. You can choose any of the 15 structures from the book.

____
____
____
____
____
____

64) Many people relapse into their sins. They really wanted to leave their sinful way of life, and they do move away from it for a while, but they never uproot or destroy the dwelling place that edified the sin in their soul.

a) True
b) False

65) Complete the blanks with key words from page 55.

The Church's main task is to edify ______________________ in each believer, not fill us with ______________________ that deny the effectiveness of God's power.

66) One of the fundamental things Jesus Christ came to restore was precisely God's dwelling in the soul and spirit of man.

a) True
b) False

67) King David penetrated the beauty and power of the dwellings of God but could not establish them in himself.

a) True
b) False

68) Explain what happens to him who builds his spiritual home in God.

____
____
____
____
____
____

69) The "will of man" is our most powerful tool to enter the Kingdom of God and His heritage, but this can be possessed by Satan.

a) True
b) False

70) Complete the blanks with key words from page 59.

You have in your ________________, the ________________to make radical decisions that will ________________to change. Some of them will require a fight, yet ____________ and only ____________decide if you will fight with ___________to __________or if you will surrender to the ____________________ to ______________________________. THE DECISION IS YOURS!

71) Mark an X by the correct answers. God is calling us:

a) ____ To be aggressive against everything that preventing us from entering the wonderful dimensions of His dwellings.

b) ____ To understand that we have a free will but the devil can take our will in our moments of weakness.

c) ____ To receive Christ into our lives, upon which moment all our iniquity is automatically deleted.

d) ____ To leave the passivity and conformism that moves on mediocrity and which is not shaming the wisdom of this world.

Check for all the correct answers in the last section of this workbook. (Page 61)

NOTES

CHAPTER 4
THE OPERATION AND MANIFESTATION OF INIQUITY

72) The body of iniquity is full of information and covenants that have accumulated from generation to generation.

a) True
b) False

73) The plan of God is not for ALL to hear His voice; ONLY the prophets or those who manifest prophetic gifts will hear His voice.

a) True
b) False

74) Complete the blanks with key words from page 62.

Jesus said, "My sheep ______________ my______________, and they ______________ me."

75) We have the power to hear the spiritual world. This is confirmed when we recognize that we hear the voice of the devil daily, receiving thoughts such as fear, anxiety, discouragement, negativity, etc ....

a) True
b) False

76) The voice of God becomes clear or is hindered by the presence or absence of iniquity.

a) True
b) False

77) Complete the blanks with key words from Isaiah 59:1-2.

Behold, the Lord's hand is not shortened, that it cannot save; neither His ear heavy, that it cannot hear: But your ________________have ______________ between you and your __________;

and your sins have hid His face from you, that He will not ______________________________.

78) Explain the meaning of a "spiritual dullness in the ear".

____
____
____
____
____
____

79) Mark the correct answer.

Maria has had 5 wonderful years in His Glory, serving the Lord in a marriage ministry. In this ministry, there are 50 leaders and each leader has a home church comprised of 30 solid marriages in the Lord. But Maria is going on 7 years of financial difficulty, unable to settle that area of her life.

The reason is:
a)___ In some part of her past or that of her ancestors there were unfair or unjust activities in the economic area and she has either forgotten or is unaware.
b)___ Her ministry is so richly blessed that it is inevitably attacked by the devil in this one area, since she cannot receive financial fulfillment.

80) Through the revelation of the gifts of the Holy Spirit, or through dreams or receiving a Words of Knowledge, we must make a detailed analysis of our works and that of our ancestors, to identify all roots of iniquity.

a) True
b) False

81) The process of rooting out all iniquity fundamentally requires assistance and participation by a minister in the church.

a) True
b) False

82) Describe the spiritual root from which all sin originates.

____
____
____
____

83) If you take the time to make a detailed list, with the help of the Holy Spirit, and ask for forgiveness for each of your actions, you will be completely free and live a life of peace.

a) True
b) False

84) Explain why iniquity produces spiritual deafness.

____
____
____
____
____
____

85) Complete the blanks from 2 Corinthians 3:16-18.

Nevertheless when it shall turn to the _____________, the veil shall be taken___________.
Now the Lord is that Spirit; and where the Spirit of the Lord is, there is __________________.

86) Mark with an X for the reasons why many people have spiritual eyes not yet opened. Use a "XX" for the main reason.

a) ___ Because of the veils of iniquity have not been removed, or the understanding from their spiritual senses.
b) ___ Because the only people that can see the riches of the glory of God are those who have a special calling in their lives.
c) ___ For some mature believers, they have not developed their spiritual vision.
d) ___ Because they have never really believed they can see in the spiritual world.
e) ___ Because they have not put the emphasis needed to be trained in these gifts.

87) Thousands of Christians have believed in Jesus as their Savior, but in many areas of their lives they are incredulous, because their hearts are still contaminated with iniquity, which has not been purged. This has resulted in their "spiritual blindness".

a) True
b) False

88) Explain how we can remove the veils that produce spiritual blindness in our lives.

____
____
____

89) Complete the blanks from what Jesus said (from page 69).

Yet a little while, and the world seeth me no more; but ye see me: because I live, ____________________. John 14:19

90) Through Jesus we are filled with the Holy Ghost, but without the power to hear and see what the Father says and does.

a) True
b) False

91) By means of iniquity, the devil has used a veil of darkness to blind the Church. Iniquity fills them with unbelief or guilt, with the sole purpose of preventing the Church from moving in the power that Jesus purchased at the cross.

a) True
b) False

92) Iniquity has its origin in the spirit of man, then travels through the soul and ends as a physical manifestation that destroys the body.

a) True
b) False

93) The condition of the spirit and soul are crucial to affect the state of the organism.

a) True
b) False

94) Complete the blanks with key words from page 71.

A spirit filled with the presence of God along with ___________________, purged and_________________, will result in a healthy body, or the health of ________________. The opposite is a body in _________________________________and prone to ______________________.

95) Write Psalm 109:18, which refers to the man who has iniquity.

____

____

____

____

96) Iniquity forms a kind of extremely toxic liquid that accumulates in the body, sits inside the bones, thus deteriorating organs and overall health.

a) True
b) False

97) Why are blood diseases such as diabetes, leukemia, high blood pressure, lupus, etc.., the product of iniquity?

____
____
____
____
____
____

98) Sadness is not from God and can cause death. Death cling to iniquity and penetrate the bones.

a) True
b) False

99) Mark with an X the diseases in bones and joints that are the result of the continuous impregnation of the secretion that comes from iniquity.

a) ___ Osteoporosis
b) ___ Arthritis
c) ___ Rheumatic pains

100) Iniquity enters in the form of "serpent eggs", creating cancerous tumors which multiply.

a) True
b) False

101) Iniquity creates within us thick "cobwebs" from the darkness, which weave into the muscles, bringing severe pain and physical decay.

a) True
b) False

102) Complete the blanks with key words from page 73.

Iniquity, as we have already seen, originates in the_______________________, and passes to his ____________________, building his structures of ___________________. Finally, this passes to the body making it ______________________________and destroying its functions.

103) All habits destructive to the human body are related to iniquity, such as vices and disturbances that may come from our past generations or developed from ourselves.

a) True
b) False

104) There is no authority or power in us to help our children be free of iniquity.

a) True
b) False

105) Consumption of drugs is another example of iniquity against the body.

a) True
b) False

106) Complete the blanks with key words from page 75.

The Word "Pharmakeia" is used in the Bible to describe _______________________________.

107) Write the meaning of Pharmakeia.

____
____
____
____
____

108) Jesus took our infirmities on the cross in the same way that He took sin and iniquity, so the true Christian should walk toward the release from drug dependence.

a) True
b) False

109) Overeating is not considered as sin, they are just pleasures and cares of life.

a) True
b) False

110) Overeating is considered iniquity and comes from a root of self destruction.

a) True
b) False

111) Iniquity within the human being, in the invisible world, traps the soul.

a) True
b) False

112) The iniquity of a person does not affect others.

a) True
b) False

113) A righteous person can be trapped by "collective" iniquity.

a) True
b) False

114) Explain how a person can be affected by the sin of another.

____
____
____
____

115) What should we do with a person with iniquity, who has changed his/her way of life for the better, but his/her soul is bound in the past?

____
____
____
____
____
____
____
____

116) Which Psalm states that King David has been beset by evil, iniquity has been cast upon him, and his soul has gone into captivity?

117) What are the causes that lead the soul into captivity?

118) Prisons of darkness are produced by people with iniquity who hurl towards us curses and hatred.

a) True
b) False

119) Souls who do not give glory to God may also be trapped in captivity.

a) True
b) False

120) Explain how you remove a soul from a pit of captivity.

121) Explain what happens when the Lord gives us authorization and revelation to release a soul from bondage.

122) The torrents of perversity are, in the spiritual world, pits which one can get out from with prolonged fasting.

a) True
b) False

123) The torrents of perversity are spiritual swamps sent by the devil to devastate a person.

a) True
b) False

124) The torrents of perversity are iniquities of others that affect only the righteous, oppressing them until they literally feel like they are drowning.

a) True
b) False

125) Explain how we are able to break free of these torrents.

____
____
____
____
____

126) Write Isaiah 59:20-22

____
____
____
____
____

127) The fall of Satan is closely linked to commerce and wealth.

a) True
b) False

128) There an element of trade, commerce and wealth, that is just and necessary for the peoples of the earth.

a) True
b) False

129) Complete the blanks with key words from page 88.

Commerce and riches project such a __________, that they have become the door for ____________________________. This splendor is a glory that is ____________________________.

130) The power of material prosperity in abundance puts us in the right place at par with God.

a) True
b) False

131) From the beginning of time, man has sought gold more than he has sought God.

a) True
b) False

132) Commerce has been steeped in iniquity in every way possible, and to a greater or lesser extent this is a constant issue in the bloodline for most men.

a) True
b) False

133) Gold has been sought to be given as an offering of worship to God.

a) True
b) False

134) Complete the blanks with key words from page 89.

All kinds of satanic covenants, witchcraft and high magic surround the ________________. The most abominable crime organizations have originated from love and ________________.

135) For many in the Church, it is more of a priority to sacrifice to obtain the riches of this world than to sacrifice their lives to achieve higher levels in God.

a) True
b) False

136) Describe what happens to us when our possessions, our salaries or our businesses have become our security and not God?

____

137) Cite three examples from this teaching on how iniquity in our systems of the world are full of filth, fornication, theft, lying and falsehood.

138) In churches, people are robbing God in tithes and offerings and the one who lacks justifies lying and cheating their brother.

a) True
b) False

139) Explain what happens when we shelter ourselves with money and riches and how we are signing a "pact" with death. Include which verse in Psalms reveals this truth.

140) Reliance on wealth is just something that is attributed only to the rich and powerful.

a) True
b) False

141) Complete the blank with key words from page 92.

Financial iniquity attracts itself to ________________________________.

142) How can we know if we have financial iniquity in our generational line?

____
____
____
____
____
____

143) Explain what can be done if the Lord reveals there is financial iniquity in our generational line.

____
____
____
____
____
____
____

144) From the day I'm free of financial iniquity, God will return what has been stolen and the blessings of the Lord will remain on my life.

a) True
b) False

145) It is important to analyze the origin of all commercial activity and detect possible sources of iniquity that would bring eventual ruin.

a) True
b) False

146) Some Christians think God wants to bless them financially regardless of the means so they shield themselves under Proverbs 13:22 and conduct ungodly business believing their are free from financial iniquity.

a) True
b) False

147) Financial iniquity can result in God not hearing our prayers.

a) True
b) False

148) The teaching tells us of two cases of financial transactions that seem noble and common, but their origin is wicked. Choose the one that surprised you the most and explain it.

____

____

____

____

____

____

149) Complete the blanks with key words from page 96.

God wants to give us abundant blessings and he will, as soon as we become the _______________ to help our ____ solve their problems.

150) Explain how we climb out on iniquity of scarcity and financial ruin.

____

____

____

____

____

151) It is through our humility God molds us and uses us as He wills.

a) True
b) False

152) A stubborn person is one who turns his own opinion into an "idol".

a) True
b) False

153) Complete the blanks with key words from page 96.

For rebellion is as the sin of __________________________________, and stubbornness is as ____________________________________ and ______________________________________.

154) Iniquity is the foundation of curses and destruction of cities.

a) True
b) False

155) Mark an X by the elements that lead to iniquity and desolation of cities.

a) ___ Territorial consecration to pagan gods
b) ___ Masonic designs
c) ___ Movies and theaters
d) ___ Magical geometry
e) ___ Animal sacrifices and bloodshed

156) In the same way that iniquity digs holes to trap the souls, entire cities are submitted and sunken in darkness, violence and corruption.

a) True
b) False

157) Iniquity also comes from our culture, rooted in the soul and spirit of the nation.

a) True
b) False

158) Mark an X by the situations where we are making a pact with the devil.

a) ___ Calling good evil, and evil good
b) ___ Accepting as part of the culture any abominable rituals and traditions
c) ___ Witnessing the sunset at 5:30 PM
d) ___ Buying decorations for our homes, or as a gift, with shapes from ancient civilizations that represented pagan gods or demons

159) Describe in your own words how we can be free of cultural iniquity.

____
____
____
____
____

160) Complete the blanks with key words from page 102.

Religions are loaded with________________for they are deeds of death. Any religious stem is, by essence, Babylonian and is opposed to_________________________________.

161) To be free of religious iniquity, it is enough to leave behind the practice.

a) True
b) False

162) The person with religious iniquity has pacts with pagan gods disguised as virgins and saints, and drinks the cup of their abominations.

a) True
b) False

163) Verbally abusing and dishonoring a person is an injustice, a major offense and source of iniquity.

a) True
b) False

164) Iniquity can be manifested via the tongue.

a) True
b) False

165) Mark an X by the characteristics that identify a person full of iniquity.

a) ___ Careless about their speech
b) ___ Often curses
c) ___ Dresses in dark colors
d) ___Causes divisions and often offended
e) ___ Negative people, full of anger and bitterness

166) People who have been abused are constantly attracting outrage and shame over their lives. They are victims of injustice, and become like a magnet that attract more injustices.

a) True
b) False
167) Describe what happens with iniquity in a case of incest.

____
____
____
____
____

168) Complete the blanks with key words from page 106.

In order to stop this cycle of injustice and affront, one must inquire in his or her___________________, identifying those occasions when we have been _______________towards other people. Then, if you do not know the instance where this sin and iniquity originated ask for___________________. Also, ask God for forgiveness for the iniquity of your_____________________________________.

169) To end the iniquity of abuse and injustice in our lives all we have to do is repent before God.

a) True
b) False

170) To end the iniquity of abuse and injustice, it is necessary to ask for forgiveness and restitution may be necessary.

a) True
b) False

171) A type of iniquity highly despised by God is the worship of idols, to bow and serve other gods. In Latin America and Europe, these are gods are invisible, such as money, food and culture.

a) True
b) False

172) In North America idols are represented by graven images only.

a) True
b) False

173) Complete the blanks with key words from page 107.

Unfortunately, ____________________is the beginning of a series of sins directed by the spirit of ___________________________________.

174) Today, in many Christian churches there is a proliferation of sins of adultery, pornography and fornication. The people of God have lost fear of Him.

a) True
b) False

175) The spirit of fornication prevents the believer from knowing God fully.

a) True
b) False

176) Complete the blanks with key words from page 108 (Hosea 4 and 5).

Whoredom and wine and new wine take away ________________. My people ask counsel at their stocks, and their staff declareth unto them: for the spirit of __________________hath caused them to err, and they have gone _________________________from under their God.

177) It is important to uproot iniquity thoroughly and accurately, for where there has been idolatry, the spirit of fornication is unleashed.

a) True
b) False

178) Fornication is related only to physical issues.

a) True
b) False

179) The iniquity and spirit of fornication continually persecute the victim with dreams and perverse thoughts.

a) True
b) False

180) Explain how we can be free from the iniquity of fornication.

____
____
____
____
____

181) Once the work of liberation is complete, it is important to declare freedom over our descendants.

a) True
b) False

182) Both blessings and curses are spiritual lasws searching for a place to land, like a bird in flight trying to find a place to nest in order to establish himself and fulfill his purpose.

a)True
b)False

183) Explain why there are many cases of people who have studied about curses, revoked and canceled them in their lives, but they keep coming back over them.

184) Complete the blanks with key words from page 111.

Sin, ________________ and _______________ require observation and an exhaustive analysis of our ________________________________.

185) In the sincere prayer of conversion unto Jesus, many sins where not confessed, yet we receive our salvation. Meanwhile, the Holy Spirit begins to reform our conscience by showing and giving us an understanding of all the sin in our lives and leading us to repentance for sins, even for sins we were ignorant of.

a) True
b) False

186) It is necessary to identify, through prayer, the root of iniquity that has produces curses in our lives.

a) True
b) False

187) Complete the blanks with key words on page 113.

A curse is the ______________ given by _________________________ to a __________________ and to his ____________________________ as a result of their _________________________.

188) Describe how we can identify curses in our lives.

____
____
____
____

189) Order the following points in the sequence, from first to last, required to cancel and revoke a curse in our lives.

a)___ Identify the causes of the curses
b)___ To proclaim the victory of Jesus on the cross for our lives, where He became a curse to set us free. (Galatians 3:13 -14)
c)___ Repent of iniquity why these curses are recurrent
d)___ Revoke and cancel the curses, breaking their power over their lives

190) Practical Exercise:

The following is an theoretical case of a woman who has recognized and severed the iniquity which, until now, has been disturbing her . Now she faces the challenge to cancel and eradicate curses that still operate in her life.

a) ____ Identify the causes of the curses in this case
b) ____ Identify the problems that these curses have brought to life with this woman
c) ____ Choose one of the curses and write (in detail) the process of cancelling and revoking these, and therefore, breaking the power of evil over her life.

-Laura is a Christian woman, she and her family have served the Lord for 5 years. His parents, both Christians, were divorced 20 years ago. Both parents are now happily married, for the second time.

-Laura's marriage is characterized by many arguments, and these have not led to divorce since they view themselves as Christians, and want to stay faithful to the Word.

-Laura was abused and raped at 16 years of age. Laura's grandparents are non practicing Catholics. Her grandmother practices witchcraft, santeria, and she curses frequently.

-Eight years ago, both Laura and her husband were heavy consumers of pornography.
-Through a dream, Laura received a revelation in which she saw her mother going to a clinic to have an abortion, which Laura later corroborated through her father.

Check for all the correct answers in the last section of this workbook. (Page 61)

CHAPTER 5
THE POWER OF ATTRACTION OF SPIRITUAL FORCES

191) Which is the spiritual force that aligns all things in the kingdom of God?

____

Which is the opposite spiritual force that tries to twist and pull apart the designs of God?

____

192) Righteousness attracts the kingdom of heaven and all the blessings from above, pulling the spiritual and material wealth for our lives.

a) True
b) False

193) Describe what needs to happen for the glory to exercise its power to attract blessings and attributes of the kingdom of heaven upon us.

____
____
____
____
____
____

194) The anointing is what takes us deep into what God is, it is the consuming fire of God; the anointing burns and destroys all that keeps us from the Lord.

a) True
b) False

195) The glory of God is the ability to fill us with joy and love.

a) True
b) False

196) We can enter the dimensions of the glory of the Lord without having rooted out and identified in our Iniquity.

a) True
b) False

197) Without the glory of God and His righteousness, we will never possess the inheritance of blessings, power and all the of wonderful additions which are found in His kingdom.

a) True
b) False

198) Righteousness and the glory of God upon our lives bring judgment on our enemies.

a) True
b) False

199) Complete the blanks with key words from page 123.

Wherever iniquity in found, we will continuously find God's judgements ______________________
____.

200) Iniquity draws darkness from the empire of death and God's judgments.

a) True
b) False

201) Explain which are the judgments of mercy from page 125.
____
____
____
____
____

202) Blessings, honor and riches come to us after being baptized.

a) True
b) False

203) Our victories depend on establishing the righteousness of God over us.

a) True
b) False

204) In what book, chapter and verse in the Bible, does it clearly show that Jesus wants to do a perfect work in us, and where it is necessary to be wash and polished by Him?
____
____

205) Complete the blanks with key words from page 127.

It is ___________________________ to have the _____________________ of God and to participate in His_________________without being first confronted with our _____________________________.

Check for all the correct answers in the last section of this workbook. (Page 61)

NOTES

CHAPTER 6
TRUE JUSTIFICATION FREES US FROM INIQUITY

206) One of the most important things God is restoring in these times, is spreading the true gospel of Jesus Christ, in all His power and glory.

a) True
b) False

207) Complete the blanks with key words from page 131.

Justification through faith originates when I ____________________________with all my _______________ that Jesus took my sins on the cross and I put my _____________ on that cross to live for _____________: when I make the_____________ to leave my old way of living behind because I am truly __________ and ________ of all the deeds that made _______________ go through a ______________ and _____________ sacrifice.

208) It is common within the church to believe that we are justified by grace and we will enter the kingdom of heaven regardless of what we do.

a) True
b) False

209) The only way to enter into the kingdom of heaven is by way of the cross.

a) True
b) False

210) Explain the meaning of the words to "invoke the name of Jesus Christ."

____
____
____
____
____
____
____

211) We must move beyond the practice of sin, with a contrite soul, and a firm intention of starting a new life.

a) True
b) False

212) According to 2 Timothy 2:19, we can invoke the Lord's name while living in iniquity?

a) Yes
b) No

213) We are immediately sealed by the Spirit upon invoking the name of the Lord, and repeating a prayer to accept Christ into our lives, even if we have not repented.

a) True
b) False

214) The mind is the mechanism with the inner strength to initiate and propel a change of direction in our lives. The heart reflects and accepts, but lacks the power to break patterns of behavior.

a) True
b) False

215) When Jesus is manifested in the heart of a true believer who has invoked His name, Christ is lifted in power to undo all iniquity, and the works of the devil.

a) True
b) False

216) When Christ manifests Himself in the heart of a true believer iniquity is purged immediately, leaving the believer free from all iniquity.

a) True
b) False

217) Believers who want to be both in the "world" and in the kingdom of heaven have never been transported from the kingdom of darkness into light.

a) True
b) False

218) In many cases today fornicators, adulterers, homosexuals, cheaters, thieves, as well as people full of pride, pornography, abuse and fraud are labeled "born again Sons of God".

a) True
b) False

219) In many cases today, we call people baptized in the Holy Spirit, even though they are still living a life with lust, deceit, witchcraft and idolatry. These people have no problems in slandering and defaming the precious Body of Christ.

a) True
b) False

220) Write 1 Corinthians 6:9-10.

____

____

____

221) Complete the blanks with key words from page 140.

The primitive church grew in the ___________ of ___________ and his ______________. They _________ what Jesus did for them, living in such a way that Jesus was glorified.

222) The justice of God is fulfilled in the believer, when the believer leaves the carnal life of sin, and lives in the Spirit.

a) True
b) False

223) Briefly explain briefly how we can identify the Spirit of God is within a person.

____

____

____

____

____

224) Complete the blanks with key words from page 141 and ROMANS 8:9.

But ye are not in the ___________, but in the __________, if so be that the Spirit of God _________. Now if any man have not the ______________, he is none of ______________.

225) Mark the correct answers with an X.

Being led by God means:
a) ___ Hearing His voice in our conscience
b) ___ Hearing His voice in His Word
c) ___ Hearing His voice in our dreams or in a prophetic word
d) ___ Having, as an anchor in life, the "Fear of God"

226) Salvation lies in man's response to the sacrifice of Christ, truly giving his life to be transformed by Christ's power.

a) True
b) False

227) Salvation is accomplished in us when we surrender our lives, with a sincere heart, on the cross.

a) True
b) False

228) Because of differences of the heart, each individual has a different timing when it comes to salvation.

a) True
b) False

229) In Galatians 5:24 we learn that those who belong to Christ will crucify their flesh little by little, as God deals with them.

a) True
b) False

230) The Bible makes a substantial difference between being "a sinner" and "an immature Christian."

a) True
b) False

231) All sin is dirty to the soul and spirit, but there are "deadly sins" and "sins of immaturity."
a) True
b) False

232) In which book, chapter and verse does God make it clear that there are "sins that lead to death" and "sins of immaturity."

233) Explain what it means to "live by the Spirit".

234) Jesus never compromised His principles to win souls and have more followers.

a) True
b) False

235) Give an example of a book, chapter and verse in the bible where Jesus did not "accommodate" the gospel to win over a soul.

236) According to page 148, what is the mission of Jesus Christ?

237) The only thing that can reconcile man with God is that Christ resurrects man's spirit.

a) True
b) False

238) Being a new creature in Christ is to be accepted as a member of a church, a change of religion or denomination, a change of behavior and morality, leaving the friends who live in the flesh, and taking courses on Christian education.

a) True
b) False

239) Complete the blanks with key words from page 151.

The new creation is the _______________ of our _______________. It is not what we may do _______________ but what we ____________. The conversion is not the adoption of a new ___________ but a complete _________________ in the ________________of our ____________.

240) A new creation is the spiritual structure formed by the divine.

a) True
b) False

241) The spirit of the natural man is dead because of sin.

a) True
b) False

242) The soul is the means or tool the spirit relates through to function in the spiritual world.

a) True
b) False

243) The soul is the most powerful part of man.

a) True
b) False

244) The eternal part of man is his soul.

a) True
b) False

245) The body was created to be the means of interpretation between the natural world and the spiritual, the soul being what governs our being.

a) True
b) False

246) It is in the spirit where the bridge between God and men is established.

a) True
b) False

247) The soul has no life, it is only an instrument to function in the animal and material world.

a) True
b) False

248) Men was created to be governing SPIRIT.

a) True
b) False

249) Salvation and new birth take place through an intellectual mechanism that passes through the heart.

a) True
b) False

250) To have a new birth and salvation, the spirit must be engendered by the Spirit of God.

a) True
b) False

251) God sows the precious seed of life in us when, with a sincere and contrite heart, we give ourselves to God and are baptized.

a) True
b) False

252) Complete the blanks with key words on page155.

It is in the ___________where the ___________of our spirit with God's Holy Spirit takes place, and a new spiritual ___________ is ___________ and starts growing in God's__________. God's life in us is in the ________________. All the power Jesus Christ arose Him from death is now what ________________ in our ____________________.

253) When we are a new creature, all the power that raised Jesus Christ from the dead will be what lives in our spirit.

a) True
b) False

254) Complete the blanks with key words from page 158.

The new creation is not a manifestation in the ___________, but in our ____________, which is transformed by the ____________________________________.

255) From pages 158-159, describe what happens to the believer who is begotten in spirit with the very life of God.

____

____

____

____

256) The resurrection is the power that gives life to this new creation that has been engendered within us.

a) True
b) False

257) From page 159, explains why the spirit of millions of people in the church sleeps.

____

____

____

____

258) Explain what is iniquity.

____

____

259) Uprooting iniquity takes time and dedication.

a) True
b) False

260) Order the following steps (from 1 to 9), of the process of releasing iniquity.

1) ___Cancel the curses that have led to iniquity in your life.
2) ___ Confess your iniquity and that of your ancestors.
3) ___ Order out of our bodies the physical substance that caused the iniquity and is lodged in your bones and organs.
4) ___ Pray for a true spirit of repentance, so you can see your iniquities.
5) ___ Consecrate the time of your conception.
6) ___ Take a notebook and write thoroughly and detailed, all that the Lord shows you regarding iniquity in your life. This process may take more than one day.
7) ___ Ask the Holy Spirit to help you in this process of liberation.
8) ___ Pray over the sins written in your notebook and those written in the bible, one by one, with a deep conviction of sin. Then confess your iniquity and the iniquity of your ancestors.
9) ___ Order the uprooting of all sin, wickedness and iniquity from your soul and spirit, ordering it to leave.

261) Iniquity may leave our bodies via fluids in the form of diarrhea, vomiting, urine, spit, and/or abundant mucus as in a cold.

a) True
b) False

262) It is convenient that once we have ordered the removal of the substance that caused iniquity, touch ourselves in every joint, and put our hands over different parts of our bodies.

a) True
b) False

263) It is essential that a person who is full of the Holy Spirit put his or her hands on each joint of vertebrae on your back, while he or she orders out the iniquity.

a) True
b) False

264) Releasing iniquity is a requirement for salvation.

a) True
b) False

265) List the sins found on pages 164 to 170. Allow the Holy Spirit to speak to you through this list.

266) Sincerely pray your final prayer and receive your deliverance.

Check for all the correct answers in the last section of this workbook. (Page 61)

NOTES

ANSWERS

INTRODUCTION

1. a)
2. c)

CHAPTER 1: WHAT IS INIQUITY?

3. a) c) d) f)
4. a)
5. b)
6. a)
7. b)
8. a)
9. a)
10. a)
11. a)
12. c)
13. a)
14. c)
15. a)
16. b)

17. Generic, Specific, Hearts, Use against us

18. a)
19. a)

20.

a) Voluntary Iniquity - With all knowledge and desire to practice evil

b) Conscious Iniquity - Root of all sins committed that still tempt us

c) Unconscious Iniquity - Difficult to detect. Can come from past gernerations causing disease and other calamity.

21. a)
22. a)
23. a)

24.
a) Intuition
b) Mind of the Spirit
c) Communion
d) Seat of Power
e) Conscience
f) Spiritual Senses
g) Inheritance

Comments

CHAPTER 2: THE CONFLICT BETWEEN THE TWO SEEDS

26. One is the fallen demonic seed, and the other divine, Jesus.

27. b)
28. a)
29. a) c) d) e)
30. a)
31. a)
32. a)

33. It is about developing each area of our spiritual being. It is a supernatural walk, guided entirely by the Spirit of God, it is the visible manifestation of Christ in us and the total destruction of the body of sin that we know is called iniquity.

34. The Spirit of God, Spiritual Life, Intimacy

35. RELIGION CANNOT DEAL WITH THE INTERNAL PART OF OUR BEING, WHERE INIQUITY LIES. THE DEVIL'S PLAN IS TO PERMEATE THE CHURCH WITH RELIGIOSITY, SO AS TO CONTROL IT BY INIQUITY, AND THUS, KILL THE LIFE OF THE SPIRIT.

36. Praying in the flesh, fake worship, carrying out the service in church while our minds are on our own thoughts.

37. a)
38. a)

39. Walking after the flesh, versus after the spirit.

40. a)

41. Keep us focused on the world

42. b)

43. Do not mind the things of the flesh, Death, Life and peace, Enmity

44. a)
45. a)

Comments

CHAPTER 3: THE DWELLINGS OF INIQUITY

46. a)

47. Intelligence, Counsel, Power, Fear of God

48. Free will

49. a)
50. b)

51. Inferior, carnal, arrogant, sinful, limited and fearful thoughts which would become the material over which the soul would Guild its spiritual habitat.

52. Psalm 84:10

53. a)
54. a)
55. a)

56. Spiritual, Mental, Emotional, From God

57. a)
58. a)
59. b)

60. By the power of God
By our determination and faith to demolish them
Changing lies for the God's unlimited truth
Beginning to think differently about ourselves
With a deep and sincere prayer when we receive Christ in our lives
Submitting our will to God
Seeing ourselves in the grandeur and power with which God sees us, and acting in this way, without doubt
Recognizing that these structures of Iniquity reside in us, and are controlling our lives
Asking a minister on a Sunday in church, to lay hands on us and pray

61. (See page 21 for list)

62. This person will live on limited finances. Regardless of how much he sows into the Kingdom of God, will never prosper. This is because his soul is surrounded by structures that attract poverty around him.

63. N/A

64. a)

65. God's dwelling place, Bible verses

66. a)
67. a)
68. N/A
69. b)
70. Free will, Power, Lead, You, Only you, God, Win, Devil, Lose
71. 1)

Comments

CHAPTER 4: THE OPERATION AND MANIFESTATION OF INIQUITY

72. a)
73. b)

74. Hear, Voice, Follow

75. a)
76. a)

77. Iniquities, Separated, God, Hear

78. It is when there are areas where a person has been treated by God in a specific area, and direction is clearly heard. But there is conflict in other areas, and the person does not know how to solve them.

79. a)
80. a)
81. b)
82. N/A
83. a)

84. Because our iniquities have a division between us and God, causing us to not hear the voice of God, in the areas of our lives that are contaminated by Iniquity. This is where there is a "Spiritual dullness in the ear" and can not hear His voice.

85.
86. a) XX
    c) X
    d) X
    e) X

87. a)

88. (From page 69)
We must identify areas of our heart that are not yet surrendered to the Lordship of Christ, through spending time with the Lord, and manifesting the presence of the Holy Spirit who can transform us, so the veils will be removed.

89. Ye shall live also

90. b)
91. a)
92. a)
93. a)

94. Pure heart, Free from iniquity, The kingdom, Pain, Sickness

95. As he clothed himself with cursing as with his garment. So let it enter his body like water, And like oil into his bones.

96. a)

97. Because iniquity affects the quality of the blood. According to the bible, blood is life, and bone marrow is where blood is made.

98. a)
99. a) b) c)
100. a)
101. a)

102. Spirit of man, Soul, Behavior, Sick

103. a)
104. b)
105. a)

106. Witchcraft

107. Pharmakeia is an Iniquity that mines the body's cells and renders the immune system useless.

108. a)
109. b)

110. a)
111. a)
112. b)
113. a)

114. The iniquity of the person is transferred to another almost as a bucket of mud, through harsh words, threats, slander, evil words, unjust accusations and pressures of all kinds, and has the effect of making the affected person literally feel like he/she is drowning.

115. We must be liberated.

116. Psalm 55:2-5

117. The soul is taken captive for reasons of Iniquity, but also due to trauma, or strong attacks by evil people which result in fragmentation of the soul.

118. b)
119. a)

120. The way to free a soul of these wells in captivity, is first to recall that everything has to be guided by the Holy Spirit. We must ask God to let us free the soul from these places and show us by His Spirit, what has caused this captivity.

121. The Lord will show through the gifts of the Spirit as to what caused this captivity. Then we will have to ask forgiveness for sin, Iniquity or rebellion. We will forgive those who have harmed the person. Finally, we order the captive soul to "BE SET FREE". And, to those who dwell in the regions of darkness, we tell them to "LEAVE THE DARKNESS AND COME INTO THE LIGHT."

122. b)

123. True

124. False

125. From our position and with the Holy Spirit, we believe and allow God to awaken His Word in our mouths. We let God to anoint us, through His Word, to undo the works of the devil that are drowning us. Then the Lord then breaks these streams and rivers of perversity using our own voice to order these swamps to be dried from their origins in the depths.

126. "The Redeemer will come to Zion, And to those who turn from transgression in Jacob," Says the LORD. "As for Me," says the LORD, "this is My covenant with them: My Spirit who is upon you, and My words which I have put in your mouth, shall not depart from your mouth, nor from the mouth of your descendants, nor from the mouth of your descendants' descendants," says the LORD, "from this time and forevermore."

127. a)
128. a)

129. Splendor, Iniquity to enter, Not God's

130. b)
131. a)
132. a)
133. b)

134. Riches of this world, Quest for riches

135. a)

136. We have fallen into the same trading that made Lucifer fall.

137. The banking systems are corrupt and full of usury. The Justice systems are also corrupt, and governments sell their integrity for money.

138. a)

139. Just as the heavens exerts its power over the just and the unjust, death is also an empire that captivates and shepherds those who are subject to it through Iniquity, transgression and sin. Psalms 49:5-6 y 13 -15.

140. b)

141. Judgment of ruin.

142. Ask the Lord to reveal it to us.

143. Ask forgiveness to God for my financial iniquity and sin, and that of my ancestors, and ask to remove the curse by way of the sacrifice of Christ for my life and that of my ancestors, and their ancestors. Then I search all the areas in which I could have sinned by putting my

trust in riches, or any other sin in the area of money, and I ask forgiveness for it.

144. a)
145. a)
146. b)
147. a)

148. Buying and selling and having a business for personal gain.

149. Answers, Neighbors

150. You should confess our sins and our iniquities, and if you have wronged someone you should restore as far as possible, even though there will be cases when this is impossible. In cases you are doing something wrong, you have to straighten the course and stop doing evil, as this will eventually bring ruin upon the person and their descendants.

151. a)
152. a)

153. Witchcraft, Iniquity, Idolatry

154. a)
155. a) b) d) e)
156. a)
157. a)
158. a) b) d)

159. Each person has to repent for his nation and purge you're his/her life of any agreement and iniquity that is in their blood because of their culture and their race.

160. Iniquity, The one true God

161. b)
162. a)
163. a)
164. a)
165. a) b) d) e)
166. a)

167. Iniquity is so strong that it attracts all sorts of curses, such as those described in Deuteronomy 28.

168. Heart, Unjust, Revelation, Ancestors

169. b)
170. a)
171. b)
172. b)

173. Idolatry, Fornication

174. a)
175. a)

176. The heart, Whoredom, A whoring

177. a)
178. b)
179. a)

180. Take a paper and pencil and made a detailed list of idols that were worshiped by self and / or family members. Note all agreements made with these images, or spirits, and what promises or offerings were made. Only after doing this in detail, with a broken heart and contrite, can we apologize to God and order to purge the iniquity out of our lives.

At the same time, we must develop a list of all situations where there has been interaction of sex outside marriage, pornography, masturbation, incest, adultery. We must be thorough and specific. In case you do not remember the names of the people they were related, the Holy Spirit is able to remind each case, it may not do it once, but take several weeks.

181. a)
182. a)

183. The reason for this is because the power of the Holy Spirit has put the curses aside for a while, but the cause of the curse was never uprooted, which is the Iniquity. They took the curses out of their lives, but not the root of why the curse entered. The curses then come back, even more powerful than before.

184. Rebellion, Iniquity, Heart

185. a)
186. a)

187. Penalty, God, Person, Descendants, Iniquity

188. We can identify them through various recurrent symptoms that come from specific roots of iniquity

189. 2) Identify the causes of curses
4) To proclaim the victory of Jesus on the cross for our lives, where He became a curse for free (Galatians 3:13 and 14)

1) Repent of Iniquity why these curses are recurrent
3) Revoke and cancel the curses, breaking their power over their lives

190. a) The causes are divorce, abuse, rape, pornography, witchcraft, idolatry.
b) This has resulted, or will result, in some of the following problems.

As a result of divorce and pornography: gynecological issues, chronic disorders of menstruation, infertility, natural abortions, divorce, spousal disloyalty.

As a result of abuse: fungi in the skin or nails, fevers and calamities, insults and abuse of all kinds.

As a result of rape: grievances and abuses of all kinds

As a result of sorcery and idolatry: susceptibility to accidents, premature death, suicides.

c) Release of curse of "divorce and pornography"

We know that Laura has purged the Iniquity in her life in this area. Therefore we will revoke and cancel all curses which were activated in her life as a result of the curses.

Laura should take the authority which Christ has given to her, and say, from the Spirit, something like this:

In the name of Jesus, I take all authority vested in my life and I stand against every curse that came upon me because of divorce in my family and pornography. My Lord Jesus Christ has made me free from all Iniquity from these causes. I revoke any damage caused in my life and my family. I declare that these curses have no power over my life or my family. Jesus Christ redeemed me from the curse of the law by becoming the curse for me on the cross; that in Christ Jesus the blessing of Abraham might come to me, so that by faith I receive the promise of the Spirit. Amen. Amen, Hallelujah!

Comments

CHAPTER 5 : THE POWER OF ATTRACTION OF SPIRITUAL FORCES

191. a) Righteousness
     b) Iniquity

192. a)

193. Eradicate all forms of injustice of iniquity in our being.

194. b)
195. b)
196. b)
197. a)
198. a)

199. Manifested

200. a)

201. Are all those circumstances and words that God speaks to our lives, dreams and divine moments of lucidity that let us see our mistakes and rectify our ways.

202. b)
203. a)

204. Malachi 3:2-3

205. Impossible, Blessings, Glory, Iniquities

Comments

CHAPTER 6 : TRUE RIGHTEOUSNESS FREES US FROM INIQUITY

206. a)

207. Believe, Heart, Life, Him, Decisions, Repentant, Ashamed, Jesus, Terrible, Painful

208. a)
209. a)

210. It is calling the Spirit of the living God to come and live in me, joining me in my spirit, for which I should be sincerely repented of the sins in my life, even those that I could not identify, but knowing that the Spirit of God brings conviction to my life. To invoke the name of the Lord, I must admit my sinful deeds, knowing that as a result of them, Jesus went through a very cruel and painful sacrifice. I long for a new life in me, leaving my old life.

211. a)
212. NO
213. b)
214. b)
215. a)
216. b)
217. a)
218. a)
219. a)

220 Scripture

221. Fear, God, Justice, Honored

222. a)

223. Because there is a total change in the thinking of man. His thirst and hunger are for the things of heaven. Never again will the things of world attract him. The seed of life in Jesus Christ will fill him with strength, fire, resurrection. He can no longer live in the flesh, but will live in the Spirit.

224. Flesh, Spirit, Dwell in you, The Spirit of Christ, His

225. a) b) c) d)
226. a)
227. a)
228. a)
229. b)
230. a)
231. a)

232. 1 John 5:16-18

233. It means staying holy, without practicing the sins of the world's sins, as a result of being led by the Spirit of God.

234. a)

235. Matthew 19:16-22

236. The mission of Jesus Christ is reconciliation with the Father, which leads us to understand how much pain is in the heart of the Father because of our sins.

237. a)
238. b)

239. Resurrection, Spirit, Religiously, Become, Philosophy, Change, Essence, Being

240. a)
241. a)
242. a)
243. b)
244. b)
245. b)
246. a)
247. a)
248. a)
249. b)
250. a)
251. a)

252. Baptism, Union, Creature, Engendered, Resemblance,Resurrection, Dwells, Spirit

253. a)

254. Flesh, Spirit, Resurrection

255. Once the Spirit is engendered an internal growth began. Every part of our spirit being is awakened and begins to develop. A new sensitivity is felt. Things we liked before, suddenly we do now. We feel removed from worldly environments. It bothers us to hear profanity, we hate sin and especially anything that grieves the Holy Spirit.

The new creation longs for things from heaven, cannot remain silent (you want to tell everyone about Jesus), and is pleased by praying and giving. The new creature is brave and loves justice, is full of fear of God and love toward neighbor.

256. a)

257. It is because of iniquity, it is like an anchor that prevents us from taking resolute steps towards God.

258. The body of sin and evil rooted in our spirit. Iniquity has corrupted the whole structure of our behavior and our thoughts, and has gotten into the bones and organs.

259. a)

260.

9) Cancel the curses that have led to Iniquity in your life.

6) Confess our iniquity and that of our ancestors.

8) Order out of our bodies that physical substance that caused the iniquity and lodged in our bones and organs.

2) Pray to bring out a true spirit of repentance, and so that we can see our iniquities.

3) Consecrate the time of our conception.

4) Take a notebook and write detailed and thoroughly, all that the Lord shows us regarding Iniquity in our lives. This process may take more than one day.

1) Ask the Holy Spirit to help us in this process of liberation.

5) With the sins in the book, pray one by one on all of them, with a deep conviction of sin.

7) Order the uprooting of all sin and wickedness from our souls and spirit.

261. a)
262. a)
263. b)
264. b)

265) List the sins found on pages 164 to 170.

266) Final prayer and deliverance

FINAL THOUGHTS OR COMMENTS

Help us to reach more people

If you want to help us promote this study with your church, family, friends, please contact us at

www.voiceofthelight.com

We want to see America free from Iniquity!

About Dr. Ana Méndez Ferrell (Author of the book, Iniquity)

With a Doctorate from the Latin University of Theology, Ana Méndez Ferrell is known internationally for her deep knowledge of the Word of God.

God has widely used her in the area of deliverance, helping millions of people to come out of the darkness of the occult, depression and generational curses affecting their lives.

Through her ministry, books, conferences and TV programs, Ana Méndez Ferrell trains and equips thousands in more than 60 nations about the true Power of God and His Authority.

Recommended books by
Dr. Ana Méndez Ferrell

-Regions of Captivity

-Iniquity

-Pharmakeia, A Hidden Assassin

-High Level Warfare, Safe from Counter Attack

-The Dark Secret of G.A.O.T.U

-Seated in Heavenly Places

-Shaking the Heavens

For free resources such as MP3s, Podcasts, Newsletters, etc., visit www.voiceofthelight.com

Voice of The Light Ministries

Visit our website

www.voiceofthelight.com

Write to:
Voice of The Light Ministries
P. O. Box 3418
Ponte Vedra, FL. 32004
United States of America

Likes us on **FACEBOOK** , follow us on **TWITTER** or watch us on **YOUTUBE** and our **Frequencies of Glory TV** channel

www.facebook.com/AnaMendezFerrellEnglishPage/ 

www.twitter.com/AnaMendezF 

www.frequenciesofglorytv.com 

www.youtube.com/user/VoiceoftheLight 

Made in the USA
Columbia, SC
22 March 2019